Messages from the Children: Every Stage is a Gift

Messages from the Children:
Every Stage is a Gift

written by Meg Flynn
MA, LMFT

artwork by Kathy Petersen

design by Massman Companies Inc.

Dedication

To everyone who has ever been a child and to everyone who gets to love a child. May we all be raised up with love and joy.

To Shawn, the love of my life, and our children, Tess and Grace, who show us the joy of life!

To my mom for her unconditional love, and being able to see the best in me and everyone.

Contents

Introduction

I hope this book inspires you to create the family life you love so that your children can grow and thrive. My goal is to offer ideas and words of affirmation that will fill the moments and rituals in your home with love, joy, and creativity. I want you to see the journey of raising your own child or the opportunity to support a child in a "Village Parenting" role of a grandparent, aunt, uncle, cousin, nanny, teacher, coach, or neighbor as a wonderful and joyful adventure to be with the magic of a child.

In each stage of a child's life, we have an opportunity to create the conditions and environment to support their developmental needs. I see each stage of a child's life as a mini-adventure of joyful discovery. The gift for the adults that love them is the opportunity to re-discover these gifts for ourselves when we join their story.

My belief is that there are no problems when it comes to children, only opportunities. Children are never the problem; they are gifts.

Any so-called problems, symptoms, obstacles, conflicts, or struggles are simply opportunities to attend to their needs with care and compassion so they can learn, heal, grow, or skill build.

When adults see children through this positive lens, we harness the power to raise healthy children. Parents, grandparents, aunts, uncles, teachers, coaches, cousins and siblings all loving a child is what creates the bond of love that is the foundation for a life of joy and possibility.

I am so excited to bring these developmental stages to life for you and to raise your awareness about the fun and opportunity of each stage. This journey starts from the first moment you dream about loving and raising a child, all the way through to the moment you release them as independent adults on their own path while cheering them on their way!

 I am Independent

 I am Accepted

 I am Smart

 I am Respected & Important

 I am Safe

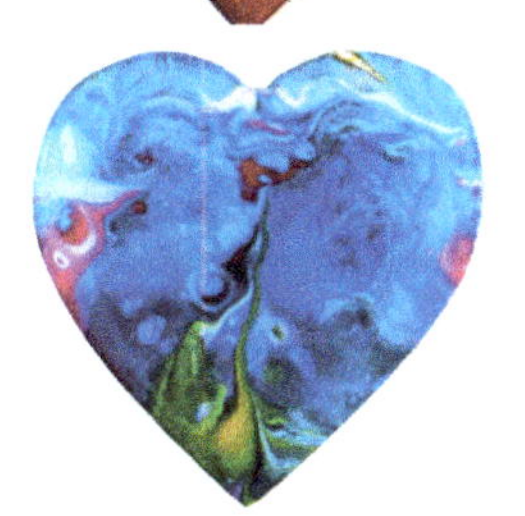 I am Loved

I AM LOVED

The Imagination Stage
preparing for loving a child

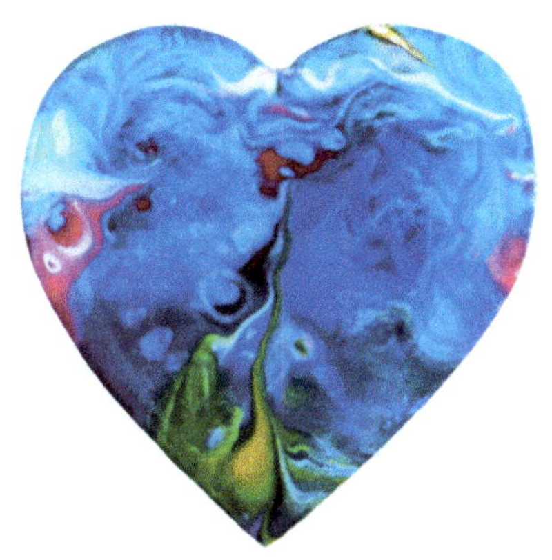

Creating your family story
The Story Matters

This is your beautiful story to create with this child.
Make it a great one!

Words are powerful, and the words you choose to
speak over yourself, your child, and your family can be
the seeds of greatness. Choose healthy, positive ways
of creating the future of your family.

In every stage, we have to pick a story and imagine how we want that stage to unfold. So often, we become afraid of something happening to our child.

For example, if you worry or fear a health concern for your child, get an exam with your trusted pediatrician because information is power. Then if all is well and the fear lingers, try to change the story with love to say, "my child is healthy, and I will take wonderful care of their body." Try to parent out of love and not fear. If you imagine a future story, pick a positive one for that stage and trust your ability to parent and guide your child through the stage successfully.

This imagination stage is so important. It is here that we create a beautiful story for the child in every stage. We imagine and visualize them joyful, healthy and happy. After that we hold this beautiful story stronger in our mind than any fear or obstacle that occurs. Then we create environments to bring that healthy story to life. The story we choose to hold and the words we speak over the child's head leads them to their best life.

I imagine a future of joy for this child

Every day I am learning to listen and care for my body with deep nurturing and awareness. This is the perfect training for how I will care for myself and the baby through all the stages.

The gift of this child in our family grows through every stage and in every stage.

I get to love this baby, and as I do, I learn to love myself more deeply.

This pregnancy and this baby are a blessing. We both deserve love and joy.

The timing of this child's life on planet Earth is in perfect alignment with their gift to all of us.

I innately know how to love my child. My skills as a parent grow as I learn and explore child development.

This pregnancy and baby are healthy.

I AM SAFE

Stage 1 - Birth-1

Self - Love
My Body Matters

This is the stage where they learn to grow their connection, safety, and trust by exploring the body of their mother/father and caregivers.

The first year is all about loving and being with your baby. Being held, feeling safe, smelling scents, hearing your voice, and feeling the motion of being walked, rocked, and swaddled are all ways in which babies bond.

The whole message is: you are loved, you are wanted, and you are safe. All you have to do is get used to being here, and we've got everything covered. Life is good. When we hold and sing to the babies, they feel so loved. This is how babies bond and learn to trust you, which eventually helps them to **trust loving relationships throughout their lives**.

Parent:

I hold and rock you
while I sing you a lullaby.
I smile and make eye
contact while I feed you.

Child:

I feel loved and connected.
I learn the gift of self-love,
which allows me to love
myself and others
throughout my entire life.

Affirmations for your child

 I am loved.

 I am safe.

 I am protected.

 I am provided with loving, gentle conditions.

 I am nurtured.

 I am cherished.

 I am given skin-to-skin time with my parents.

 I am attended to when I cry.

 I can trust my caregivers to meet my needs with love.

Self-Love

Loving your child and giving them safe, nurturing environments imprints self-love.

I AM RESPECTED
& IMPORTANT

Stage 2 - Ages 1-3
part one - toddler

Self - Care
My Feelings Matter

This is the stage where they learn to identify their feelings, grow their body, and use their skills by exploring their environments.

The second and third year of life is setting up environments for the toddler to explore and learn that they are physically safe and emotionally respected.

This is a perfect age to start helping a child learn their feelings by simply observing them and offering gentle language, saying, "I see your face and it looks like you are sad/mad/happy/scared/calm."

Reflecting their feelings and helping them name the main feeling states of sad, mad, happy, scared, and calm is a great way to help them feel understood.

Toddlers learn through touch and play. Having a room with toys (but no breakables, outlets, or tiny toys) and an adult sitting on the floor watching is heaven for them. They understand language long before they can speak. Therefore, using respectful words and informing them about what will happen, asking if they want a hug instead of forcing touch, and giving them choices create a sense of empowerment and independence. Creating these playful spaces, observing and assisting them with boundaries and tasks is how toddlers learn to **trust their environment**.

Parent:

I respect your body with safe and healthy boundaries and teach you with patience to care for and use your body.

Child:

I learn to respect and care for my body, to set healthy boundaries, and to respect others' bodies throughout my life.

Affirmations for your child

 I am respected.

 I am told what is going to happen to my body before adults help me.

 I am learning my feelings.

 I am given time to transition.

 I am given choices and healthy boundaries.

 I am allowed to play in safe environments with child-sized furniture and toys.

 I am allowed choices for my food.

 I am given predictable rituals throughout my day.

 I am given boundaries with love and patience.

Self-Care

Respecting your child's feelings and body, and attending to their physical and emotional needs imprints self-care.

Stage 2 - Ages 3-5
part two - pre-school

Self - Confidence
My Ideas Matter

This is the stage where they learn to grow their imagination by exploring many different types of play and exploring the adults, caregivers, and children in their environment to engage their ideas.

Preschool ages from 3-5 are such a wonderful time to truly listen and see your child's personality development.

This is the time to listen to their ideas and celebrate their love of play and life because they remind us that life is supposed to be fun. You make them feel important by valuing their ideas. This is the age when they say, 'Watch me!' or 'Watch this!' Children who feel heard, seen, and admired by their parents grow up with a healthy sense of self-confidence. Also, this is an important time to help them with letters, rhyming, and reading to them to create a foundation for entering school. Being present and witnessing the magic of their discoveries, such as pouring their own juice, coloring a picture, singing a song, dressing themselves, or riding a tricycle, is how they learn to **trust themselves**.

Parent:

I take time for 15-20
minute play sessions. I
allow you to lead and
show me your ideas and
things you can do.

Child:

I feel important and
learn how to express
and use my voice.

Affirmations for your child

♥   I am important.

♥   I love to imagine.

♥   I love being read to and it's the foundation of my ability to read.

♥   I am a joy to raise.

♥   I am seen, heard, and celebrated for my ideas.

♥   I am so happy when adults sing and rhyme with me.

♥   I flourish when I get to practice my ABCs and writing.

♥   I love to play, and that is how I learn.

Self-Confidence

Listening to your child and valuing
their ideas imprints
self-confidence.

I AM SMART

Stage 3 - Ages 5-8

Self - Esteem
My Achievement Matters

This is the stage where they learn to grow their minds and achieve by exploring the school system and new conditions.

Kindergarten through third grade is a time to venture out and explore how they can achieve and learn to follow the expectations set by teachers and the school.

This is a vulnerable time for little ones because it is often their first experience with conformity, precision, and comparison. In preschool, there are more play stations, and elephants can be colored purple. First grade becomes a time when elephants are gray. Everyone has to write the same alphabet, read the same words, and solve the same math problems. Children who are read to from an early age and parents who rhyme with them often have an easier time picking up these skills. This is the first stage of feeling compared to another child's schoolwork and can shape their story of feeling smart and competent.

Spending time preparing children with reading and exposure to letters, numbers, rhyming, helping them unpack their backpacks, and asking how we can help can build their trust in their ability to learn.

Parent:

I sit with you while you do your homework. I encourage you to keep trying and reassure you that mistakes are part of the learning process.

Child:

I learn to trust my mind and my ability to learn and learning feels fun.

Affirmations for your child

 I am smart.

 I am competent.

 I am learning multiple things at this stage. Some are easy, while others are challenging.

 I am a good learner. Making mistakes is how we all learn.

 My learning ability is unique. I am gaining confidence as I practice.

 I am patient with the process of learning, and so are my caregivers and teachers.

Self-Esteem

Spending time with your child making
learning safe and fun imprints
self-esteem.

I AM ACCEPTED

Stage 4 - Ages 8-15

Self - Acceptance
My Friends Matter

This is the stage where they learn to grow their relationships by exploring their social systems and community.

The stage from 4th to 9th grade is all about creating a sense of belonging and discovering what a healthy community feels like. This is also a stage where children practice feeling acceptance and rejection.

It is helpful to create a sense of belonging within the family through the rituals and joys you practice together. This can include special meals, holiday traditions, and playtime activities such as games, music, sports, art, or nature exploration - whatever brings joy to your family. Additionally, introducing your child to various activities and allowing them to choose their favorites can create multiple opportunities for a sense of belonging. It's important to set healthy expectations, such as emphasizing that school is their main job during the day and balancing with 2-3 extracurricular activities. Our job as parents is to provide many opportunities and let our children choose what resonates with them.

When our children experience hurt from others outside the family, we may be unable to control the situation. However, this is a great opportunity to teach kids how to respond with kindness and ask for help when necessary. We can create a home environment of love and acceptance where they feel safe and supported. This helps build their trust that they are accepted and valued within the family.

Parent:

I accept you as the unique wonderful person you are.

Child:

I feel a strong sense of who I am and learn to accept myself and others.

Affirmations for your child

 I am accepted.

 I am kind to others and am a good friend.

 I enjoy being a part of healthy friend groups and a healthy community.

 I try many different sports, activities, and clubs to see what I like.

 I am unique and special in so many wonderful ways. There is only one me.

 I am open to new friends and understand that change is a part of growing.

 I can ask for help and see that as a sign of strength.

 I can say when I am hurt and stand up for myself.

Self-Acceptance

Accepting your child for who they are and offering multiple activities for discovering their gifts imprints self-acceptance.

I AM INDEPENDENT

Stage 5 - Ages 15-25

Self - Reliance
My Purpose Matters

This is the stage where they learn to grow their true self and independence by exploring the bigger world and finding their path.

10th grade through 25 years old is a time of supporting their time of independence.

This is the stage where children get to make more choices, such as choosing classes, friends, jobs, and driving a car. They also get to choose whether to move out, go to school, work, or serve our country in the military, among other options. By this time, children have heard our safety lessons and observed our choices, and hopefully, they know your family values. Now is the time for us to ask more questions instead of telling them what to do and to use logical consequences to teach them how the world works. It's a time to listen, to offer support, and to cheer them on in their successes. It is a time for healthy boundaries, high expectations, and guidance, but it is also a time to offer connection, hugs, play, help, and to be there for them when they feel scared or uncertain.

This is a great time for us to create memories for our children and to help them discover what types of people, places, and things bring them alive and what causes them stress. This is a crucial time for them to ask the question, "who am I," and we can support their self-discovery with wisdom and love, helping them **trust their true selves and their path in life.**

Parent:

I believe you can face
any challenge or
obstacle and find your
way stronger and wiser.

Child:

I learn to trust and
believe in myself.

Affirmations for your child

♥ I am independent.

♥ I make good choices.

♥ I ask questions to make informed decisions.

♥ I love my body.

♥ I can receive help when I need or seek it.

♥ I can change my mind when the conditions change or do not fit my value system.

♥ I can set boundaries and say no.

♥ I follow my inner compass with my morals and values.

♥ I am discovering the deep part of my identity by exploring the world.

♥ I choose friends wisely who mirror my values and goals.

Self-Reliance

Supporting your child as they find their goals/dreams and providing healthy boundaries imprints self-reliance.

Conclusion

I hope you see that every stage where we get to be present with a child has gifts. Of course, there will be obstacles and challenges along the way, and that's why it's important that at each stage we pick a great story to get us through the more difficult moments. I hope I have inspired you to see the joy of discovery in every part of the journey.

Tips for Parents, Teachers and Caregivers

Modeling
"Showing by Example"

There is an incredible opportunity in every stage for the adult to model the gift for the child. This is not only a benefit to the child, but to the adult as well.

Creating your Family Story

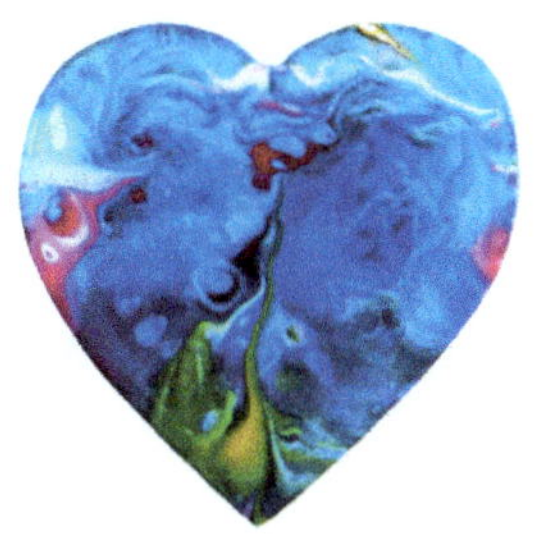

The Story Matters

When you imagine joyful
possibilities and
have the courage
to believe in you dreams, you
show your child how to
create the life they imagine.

Self - Love

When you take time to love yourself just for who you are, instead of what you do, you show your child the importance of self- love.

My Body Matters

When you care for your body with healthy physical rituals for food, sleep and exercise, your child will follow your example.

Self - Care

When you care for yourself without feeling guilty, you show your child the importance of self-care.

My Feelings Matter

When you are able to identify your feelings: happy, sad, mad, afraid, content; you teach your child how to do the same.

Self - Confidence

When you feel confident in your ideas and choices and trust your inner compass, you show your child the importance of self-confidence.

My Ideas Matter

When you follow your own ideas of joy and play, you model that life can be fun.

Self - Esteem

When you increase your
competency and skill in any area of
your life, you show your child the
importance of self-esteem.

My Achievement Matters

When you learn new things,
and ask for help, your child
sees the importance of being a
lifelong learner.

Self - Acceptance

When you look inward for approval instead of outward, you show your child the importance of self-acceptance.

My Friends Matter

When you find and nurture healthy friendships you teach your child to find joy in community.

Self - Reliance

When you practice independence
you show your child the importance
of self-reliance.

My Purpose Matters

When you find meaning and
purpose in things you hold sacred,
you show your child they can
make a difference.

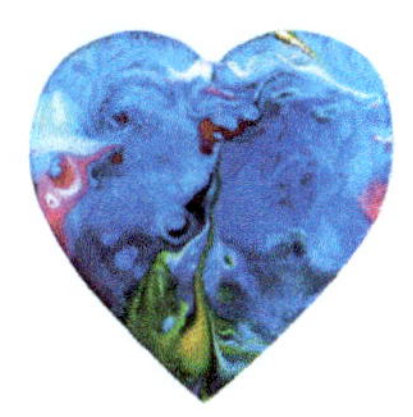

"Do not tell them how to do it.
Show them how to do it and do
not say a word. If you tell them,
they will watch your lips move.
If you show them, they will
want to do it themselves."
~ Maria Montessori

The Joy of the Journey

These stages are an
adventure we take to discover
the joy along the way.

The joy in
finding my path

The joy in
community

The joy in
learning

The joy in
play

The joy in
connection

The joy in dreaming
and imagining
a great story

Page Designed by
Tess, Age 11

The Gifts from Every Stage

Page Designed by
Grace, Age 8

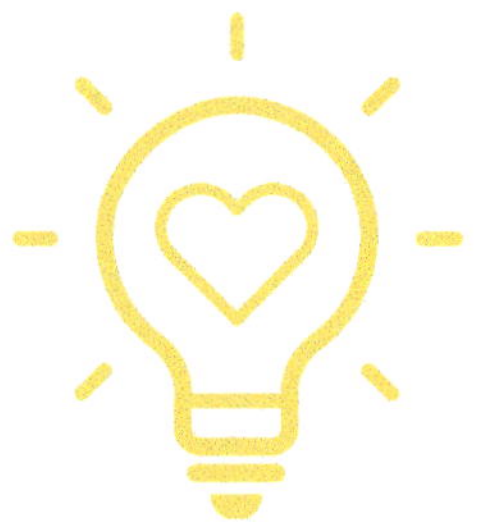

Resources

Dolly Parton's Imagination Library is a book gifting program that mails free, high-quality books to children from birth to age five, no matter their family's income.

https://imaginationlibrary.com/

Life Mapping Program
The Life Mapping program is a 10-session program designed by Meg Flynn to take people back into their personal history to understand the roots of strengths and patterns and how they impact current behaviors, belief systems and our interactions with others. It identifies and works to correct any negative patterns that may be holding the person back from optimizing their potential.

Learn more about Life Mapping on page 89.

https://www.newdirectionsct.com/life-map

About the Author

Meg Flynn has a passion for helping people create healthy families. She loves working with children and families to create meaningful communication, rituals, and joy in their lives.

With over 25 years of service to families, she is the author of "Messages From the Children: Every Stage is a Gift" and the creator of the Life Mapping leadership training program. Meg is a licensed Marriage and Family Therapist with special training in child development, holding an M.A. in Counseling Psychology from the University of St. Thomas and a graduate degree in Early Child Family Education from St. Cloud State University, as well as a B.A. in Psychology and Theology from the College of St. Benedict in Minnesota.

As the owner and director of New Directions Counseling & Training, Ltd in St. Cloud, Minnesota, Meg focuses her practice on building and strengthening family relationships. She resides in Minnesota with her husband, two daughters, and their golden doodle.

Acknowledgments

I want to first acknowledge my foundation for this work by respecting all of the pioneers in the field of developmental psychology and early childhood development, including Erik Erickson's psychosocial stages of development, Abraham Maslow's hierarchy of needs, Sigmund Freud's psychosexual stages, Jean Piaget's theory of cognitive development, B.F. Skinner and John B Watson's behaviorist theories and John Bowlby's attachment theory. I also need to acknowledge the field of family systems therapy and the field of narrative therapy for helping us understand the power of the stories we create and therefore live. Finally, thank you to Louise Hay for her teachings on the power of affirmations.

I want to thank my husband and business partner, Shawn, for every kind of support, and my smart, creative, and beautiful girls, Tess and Grace.

My parents Dorothy and Joseph, for all the gifts. My sisters Tracy, Kate, Colleen (Bean), and Ellen. My brothers Mike, Chris, and Jack. My in-laws and wonderful Grandparents and artists Kathy and Jim Petersen. To all my nieces and nephews, aunts, uncles, and cousins.

My Colleagues and fellow therapists Stefanie Okeson and Brittany Reinke. My support circle of women Sara, Emma, Karen, Tracy, Steph, Dana, Sue, Lisa, Angie, Jill, Deb, and Stacy.

My wise mentors on the journey Geno Beniek, Carol Belling, Carol Abbott, Sherry Finneman, Carol Ritberger, Mary Kay Carle, Matt Steinkamp, Jane Ellison, Glen Palm, Sr. Shaun Omeara, Skip Nolan, Mary Hayes, Chuck Smith, Darryl Goetz, Kirk Lamb, John Christenson, Ger Christenson, and Henry Christenson.

 I want to acknowledge and honor the hundreds of children and families that have trusted me and given me the privilege of being a part of their story as an early childhood teacher, parent educator, and therapist.

And finally, with such gratitude to Michelle and Gary Massman for encouraging me and believing in this from the beginning to make it possible.

Contact

Author
Meg Flynn
www.messagesfromthechildren.com

Visit our website and register to receive our email newsletter and be notified of upcoming events, workshops and training opportunities.

We would be excited to work with you! Please contact Michelle for details on the following:

Speaking and workshop presentations
Wholesale requests
Collaboration opportunities

Michelle Massman
mjmassman@aol.com

Life Mapping Program

The Life Mapping Program is a deep transformational process designed for leaders and influencers in companies, families and communities. The program will guide you through the path of your life story. Deeply understanding your past and making peace with it is the best way to create your future. When you begin the journey of going back into your story, you will discover and build upon the roots of your true strengths. You will also uncover the roots of negative patterns in your life so you can heal and overcome those unconscious parts.

- Find your authentic voice
- Re-Write old scripts
- Become more self aware
- Re-discover the deep self-care you need to be healthy and joyful
- Take time to nourish yourself
- Strengthen Core Values
- Let go of blocks from the past
- Redefine who you are as a leader
- Release old patterns
- Become the leader you were meant to be

The Life Mapping Program is not therapy. It is a 10-session program that is specifically designed by Meg Flynn to take people back into their personal history to understand the roots of strengths and patterns and how they impact current behaviors, belief systems and our interactions with others. It identifies and works to correct any negative patterns that may be holding the person back from optimizing their potential.

Personal outcomes:

- Develop the ability to interpret and understand positive and negative "scripts" from childhood based on your life experiences

- Raise your self-awareness & your ability for self-care to promote clarity and holistic health

- Embrace your strengths and gifts and your ability to leverage them for your personal wellbeing

- Increase your understanding of old, negative/limiting beliefs passed on through generational patterns

- Engage in techniques to release old patterns and replace with empowering beliefs

- Recognize roots of stress and their impact on your health, resilience, and development

Professional outcomes:

- Develop empowering techniques to stay fulfilled and passionate in your work life and optimize your potential

- Gain insight into your own leadership style

- Identify what empowers you to inspire and lead

- Notice triggers that disempower you in workplace interactions

- Learn techniques to change negative patterns

- Build awareness on how systems work & how organizational dynamics can be led with consciousness and creativity

- Develop compassion and empathy towards co-workers, employees and clients through increased psychological awareness of what motivates people

Due to the in-depth nature of this program, there are limited spots available.

To learn more or inquire about available openings, call or email New Directions Counseling & Training at 320-654-0001 / <u>newdirections@ndct.net</u>

A Place for Your Thoughts

Use this space to capture your reflections and insights inspired by the messages in this book. It's your personal area to connect, contemplate, and create.

www.ingramcontent.com/pod-product-compliance
Lightning Source LLC
Chambersburg PA
CBHW061131160726
48006CB00036B/1726